STORIES FROM
THE
JEWISH
WORLD

written by

Sybil Sheridan

illustrated by

Robert Geary

Silver Burdett Press
Morristown, New Jersey

Managing Editor : Belinda Hollyer
Book Editors : Barbara Tombs, Jenny Vaughan
Designer : Liz Black
Production Controller : Rosemary Bishop

Consultant : Angela Wood, Lecturer in Religious Studies, West London Institute of Higher Education

First published in Great Britain in 1987 by
Macdonald & Co (Publishers) Ltd
London & Sydney
A BPCC plc company

Printed and bound in Great Britain by
Purnell Book Production Ltd,
Paulton, nr. Bristol

Adapted and first published in the United States in 1987 by
Silver Burdett Press, Morristown, New Jersey

Library of Congress Cataloging-in-Publication Data
Sheridan, Sybil.
    Stories from the Jewish World.
    (Stories from the religious world)
    Summary: A collection of tales from the Jewish
faith, including the stories of Abraham, Akiva
who wanted to be a rabbi, and the golem of Prague.
    1. Legends, Jewish.   [1. Folklore, Jewish]
I. Title.   II. Series.
BM530.S485   1987   296.1'9   86-61625
ISBN 0-382-09312-7

CONTENTS

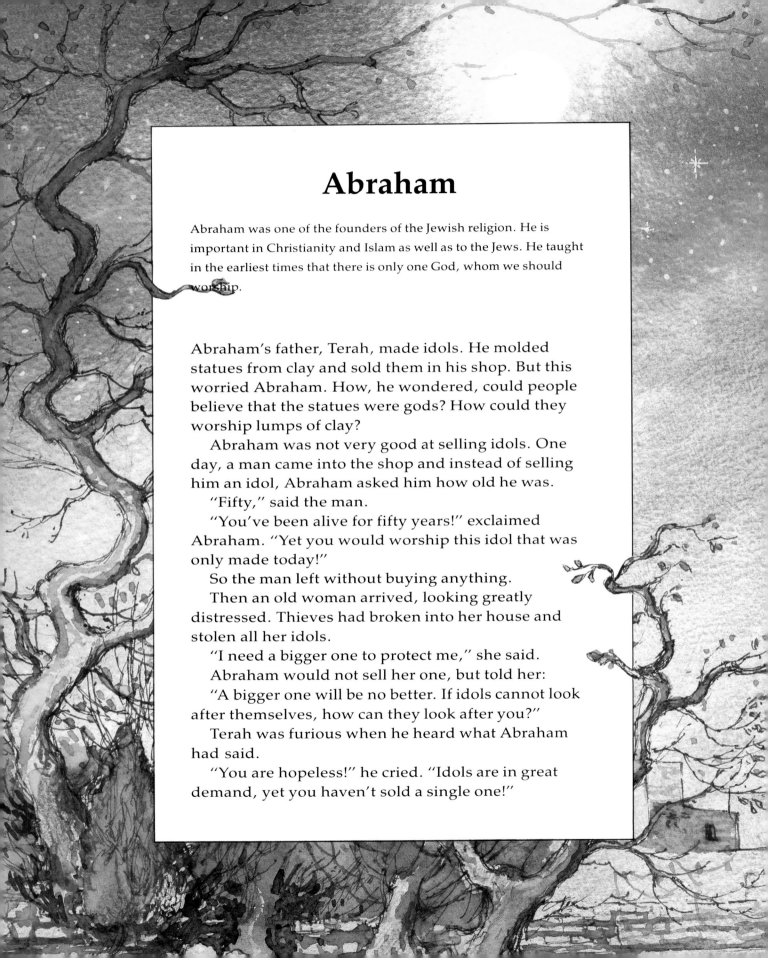

Abraham

Abraham was one of the founders of the Jewish religion. He is important in Christianity and Islam as well as to the Jews. He taught in the earliest times that there is only one God, whom we should worship.

Abraham's father, Terah, made idols. He molded statues from clay and sold them in his shop. But this worried Abraham. How, he wondered, could people believe that the statues were gods? How could they worship lumps of clay?

Abraham was not very good at selling idols. One day, a man came into the shop and instead of selling him an idol, Abraham asked him how old he was.

"Fifty," said the man.

"You've been alive for fifty years!" exclaimed Abraham. "Yet you would worship this idol that was only made today!"

So the man left without buying anything.

Then an old woman arrived, looking greatly distressed. Thieves had broken into her house and stolen all her idols.

"I need a bigger one to protect me," she said.

Abraham would not sell her one, but told her:

"A bigger one will be no better. If idols cannot look after themselves, how can they look after you?"

Terah was furious when he heard what Abraham had said.

"You are hopeless!" he cried. "Idols are in great demand, yet you haven't sold a single one!"

That night, Abraham could not sleep. He kept asking himself the question:

"How can the idols in the shop be gods, when they are only made of clay?"

He went outside. It was dark and the sky was full of brilliant stars.

"How beautiful," he thought. "So far and yet so bright. No one made them — surely they are gods."

He started to worship them — but, suddenly, the moon appeared. It was larger and brighter than the stars in the sky.

"The moon is even more beautiful than the stars and much larger," thought Abraham. "Surely it must be God."

Abraham worshiped the moon all night, but at dawn it disappeared and in the east, the sun slowly began to rise.

9

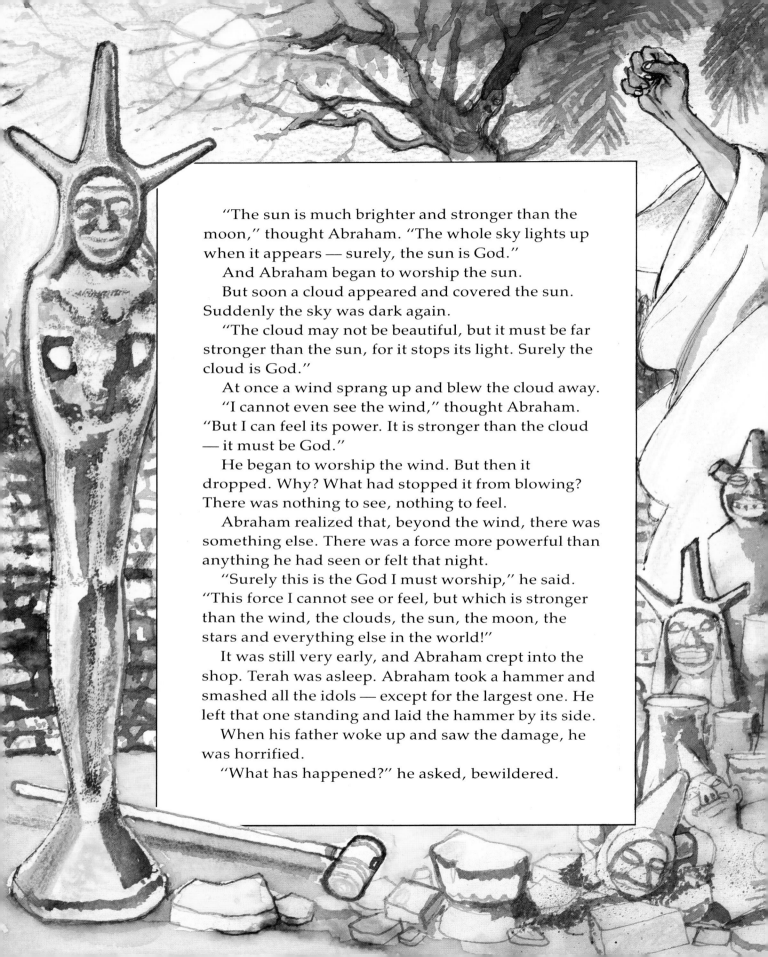

"The sun is much brighter and stronger than the moon," thought Abraham. "The whole sky lights up when it appears — surely, the sun is God."

And Abraham began to worship the sun.

But soon a cloud appeared and covered the sun. Suddenly the sky was dark again.

"The cloud may not be beautiful, but it must be far stronger than the sun, for it stops its light. Surely the cloud is God."

At once a wind sprang up and blew the cloud away.

"I cannot even see the wind," thought Abraham. "But I can feel its power. It is stronger than the cloud — it must be God."

He began to worship the wind. But then it dropped. Why? What had stopped it from blowing? There was nothing to see, nothing to feel.

Abraham realized that, beyond the wind, there was something else. There was a force more powerful than anything he had seen or felt that night.

"Surely this is the God I must worship," he said. "This force I cannot see or feel, but which is stronger than the wind, the clouds, the sun, the moon, the stars and everything else in the world!"

It was still very early, and Abraham crept into the shop. Terah was asleep. Abraham took a hammer and smashed all the idols — except for the largest one. He left that one standing and laid the hammer by its side.

When his father woke up and saw the damage, he was horrified.

"What has happened?" he asked, bewildered.

"Well," said Abraham, "The idols were quarreling and the big idol became very angry and took the hammer and smashed the others to pieces."

"Liar!" shouted Terah. "Idols can't move."

"If you don't believe me," Abraham said, "ask the big idol. He will tell you."

"Fool!" screamed his father. "Idols can't speak."

"If idols can't move or speak," replied Abraham, "how can you worship them? How can they be gods?" Terah could not answer.

Then Abraham told him of what had happened that night, and Terah too began to worship the invisible God, who had so much power.

11

The Lie and Evil Enter the Ark

Long ago the earth was corrupt and full of violence, so God arranged a flood to wipe out all the wickedness in the world. God told Noah to build an ark for his family and for two of every living creature.

One day, the Lie came to Noah and said, "It will rain soon, please may I have a ride in your ark?"

"No," said Noah, for he did not like the look of the Lie.

"Why not? You have so much space and you are welcoming all other creatures," said the Lie.

Noah did not know what to say — he had asked every type of animal to join him in the ark so he would need a good excuse to refuse the Lie. Then he thought of one.

"I am only taking pairs," he said. "If you can find a partner, you too can come on board."

The Lie went away to find a partner, but every animal he asked ran away. Nobody liked him. The days went by, and the skies got darker. The Lie knew he would have to find someone soon or the ark would leave without him.

He looked here and there and everywhere. At last he found a likely person. Her name was Evil, and she was as unpleasant as he was himself. The Lie went up to her and explained his problem.

"Will you marry me?" he asked. Evil had never had a proposal before.

"Yes," she said.

12

Hand in hand they ran as fast as they could to the ark. Rain began to fall and Noah was pulling up the gangplank as they arrived.

"Wait for us," the Lie shouted. "I have found a partner. You cannot refuse me now." Sadly, Noah let the Lie and Evil into the ark.

For forty days and forty nights it rained and the whole earth was flooded. For forty days and forty nights the Lie and Evil made themselves comfortable among the pairs of animals. Then the rain stopped and dry land appeared. Noah let down the gangplank and the animals went out, two by two. As they left the ark, God blessed them all, saying:

"Be fruitful and multiply and replenish the earth."

Everyone did so. The animals had offspring and Noah and his sons had several children. The Lie and Evil produced many little lies and evils which grew and multiplied until the earth was once again full of the wickedness that God had sought to destroy.

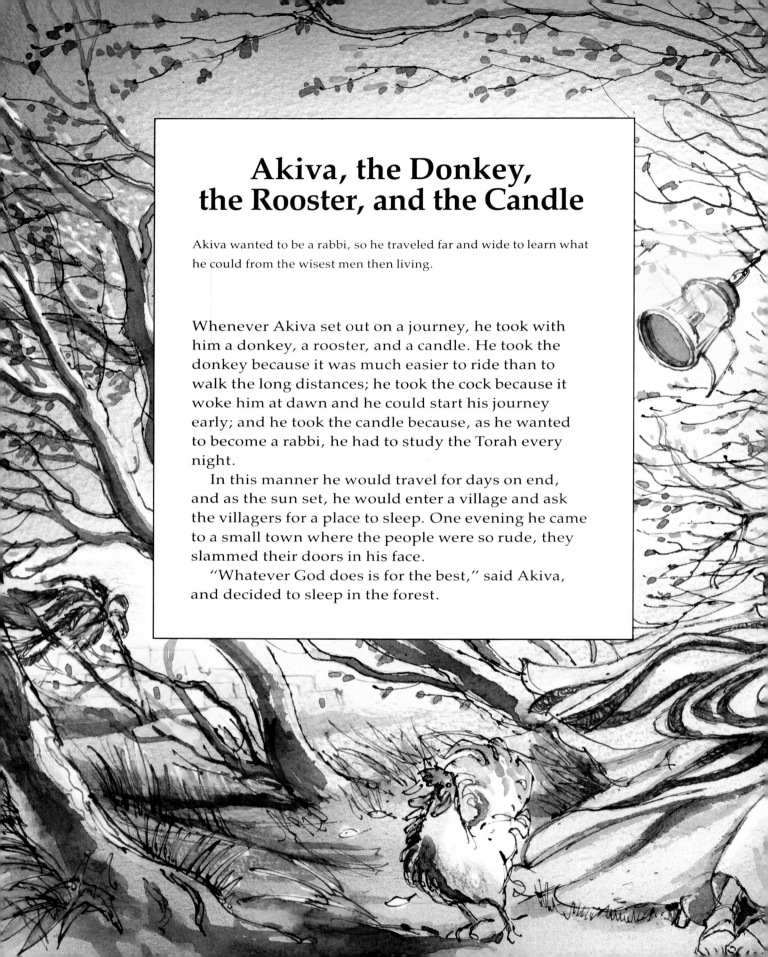

Akiva, the Donkey, the Rooster, and the Candle

Akiva wanted to be a rabbi, so he traveled far and wide to learn what he could from the wisest men then living.

Whenever Akiva set out on a journey, he took with him a donkey, a rooster, and a candle. He took the donkey because it was much easier to ride than to walk the long distances; he took the cock because it woke him at dawn and he could start his journey early; and he took the candle because, as he wanted to become a rabbi, he had to study the Torah every night.

In this manner he would travel for days on end, and as the sun set, he would enter a village and ask the villagers for a place to sleep. One evening he came to a small town where the people were so rude, they slammed their doors in his face.

"Whatever God does is for the best," said Akiva, and decided to sleep in the forest.

He found a clearing amidst the trees, settled down, lit his candle and began to study. Suddenly there was a tremendous roar and a lion leaped into the clearing and killed the donkey.

"Whatever God does is for the best," said Akiva, and went on studying. Some moments later, the rooster gave a screech and fell down dead at his feet.

"Whatever God does is for the best," he said, and turned back to his books. Then the wind blew his candle out.

"Whatever God does is for the best," sighed the poor man, and went to sleep.

The next morning he returned to the town. He could hardly believe his eyes! Every house had been burgled, every person had been killed. Robbers had come through the forest during the night and had ransacked the whole place.

Akiva sat down and thought. Had he slept in the village that night he too would have been killed. Had the robbers heard his donkey bray, his rooster crow, or seen his candle in the forest, they would surely have murdered him before they even reached the town.

"You see," he said, " whatever God does is for the best."

15

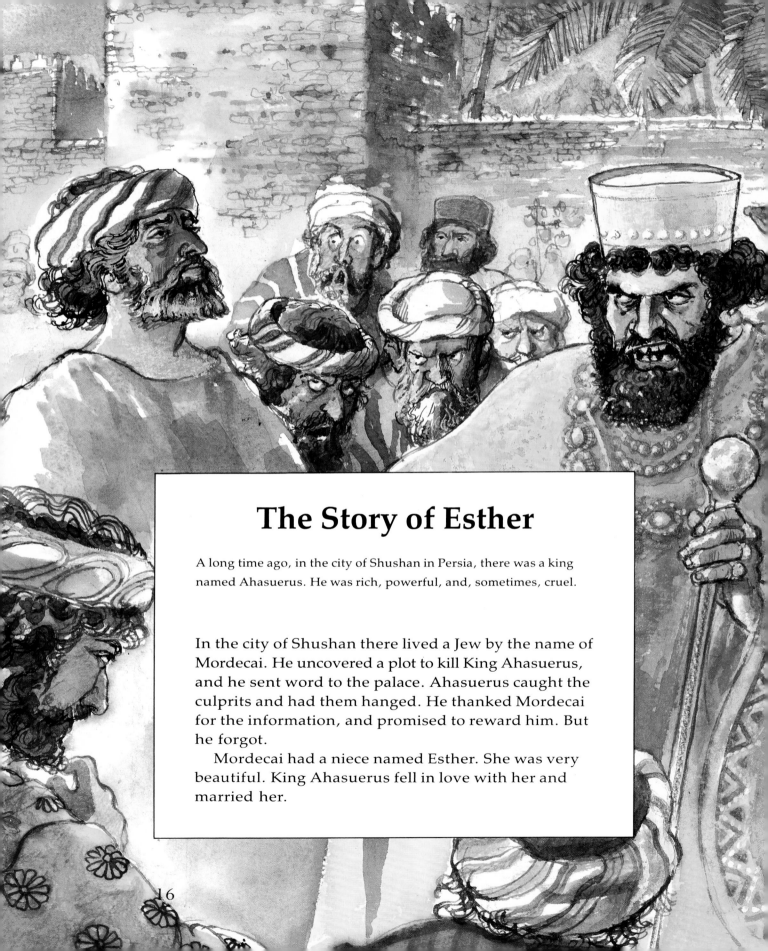

The Story of Esther

A long time ago, in the city of Shushan in Persia, there was a king named Ahasuerus. He was rich, powerful, and, sometimes, cruel.

In the city of Shushan there lived a Jew by the name of Mordecai. He uncovered a plot to kill King Ahasuerus, and he sent word to the palace. Ahasuerus caught the culprits and had them hanged. He thanked Mordecai for the information, and promised to reward him. But he forgot.

Mordecai had a niece named Esther. She was very beautiful. King Ahasuerus fell in love with her and married her.

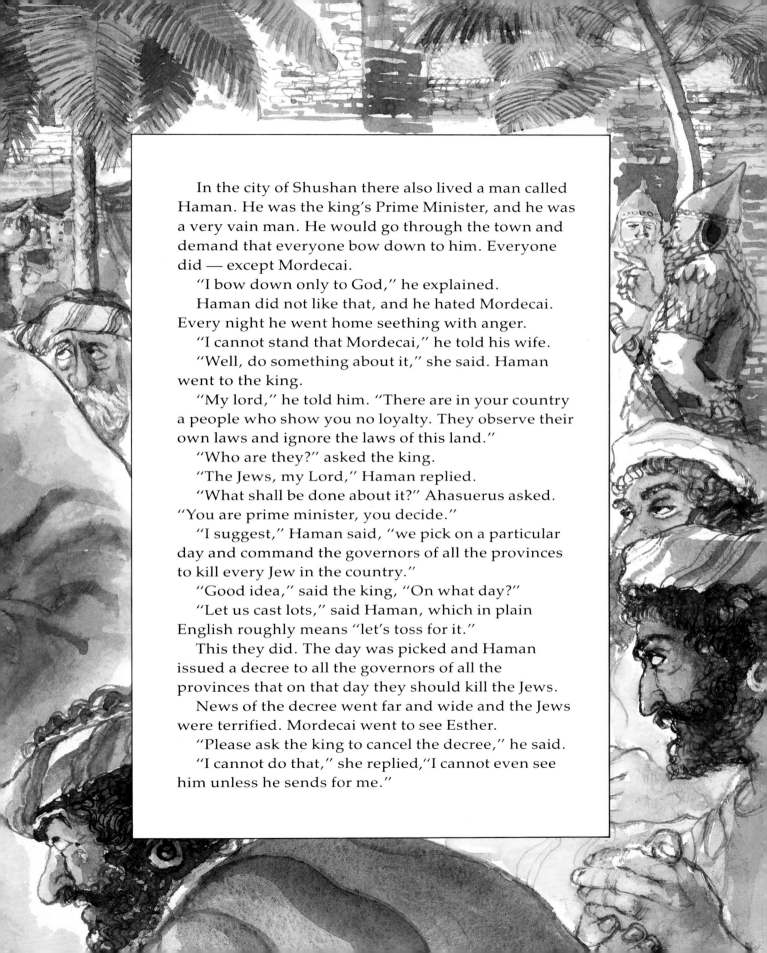

In the city of Shushan there also lived a man called Haman. He was the king's Prime Minister, and he was a very vain man. He would go through the town and demand that everyone bow down to him. Everyone did — except Mordecai.

"I bow down only to God," he explained.

Haman did not like that, and he hated Mordecai. Every night he went home seething with anger.

"I cannot stand that Mordecai," he told his wife.

"Well, do something about it," she said. Haman went to the king.

"My lord," he told him. "There are in your country a people who show you no loyalty. They observe their own laws and ignore the laws of this land."

"Who are they?" asked the king.

"The Jews, my Lord," Haman replied.

"What shall be done about it?" Ahasuerus asked. "You are prime minister, you decide."

"I suggest," Haman said, "we pick on a particular day and command the governors of all the provinces to kill every Jew in the country."

"Good idea," said the king, "On what day?"

"Let us cast lots," said Haman, which in plain English roughly means "let's toss for it."

This they did. The day was picked and Haman issued a decree to all the governors of all the provinces that on that day they should kill the Jews.

News of the decree went far and wide and the Jews were terrified. Mordecai went to see Esther.

"Please ask the king to cancel the decree," he said.

"I cannot do that," she replied,"I cannot even see him unless he sends for me."

"But you must," said Mordecai. "You are a Jew, too. Do not think that because you are queen your life will be spared."

She answered, "No one can go to the king without his permission. If, as I appear, he raises his golden sceptre, all well and good; if not, I will be executed."

Mordecai begged and pleaded and finally Esther agreed to try.

The next day, Esther dressed in her best clothes and entered the king's room. She looked so sad and so beautiful that the king immediately raised his golden sceptre and beckoned her to sit by him.

"What is it you want, my dear?" he asked. "You can have anything you like."

"All I want," she said, "is to invite you and Haman to dinner tomorrow night."

"We would be delighted," he replied.

That night, Ahasuerus could not sleep, so he decided to read from the diary he kept of all the things he did as king. He called for a servant to read the diary to him. He was just dozing off when the servant read about Mordecai. The king jumped up.

"Mordecai! My goodness, I forgot. I promised to reward him for saving my life. Call Haman at once!"

Haman appeared and asked sleepily,

"What is it my Lord wishes at this time of night?"

"Haman, what would you do to reward a man to whom you are very grateful?"

Haman, thinking the king meant him, thought of what he would like best in the world.

"You should let him wear your royal robes, give him your royal horse, let it be proclaimed that this man is very important, and make everyone bow down to him."

"Excellent!" cried Ahasuerus. "Fetch Mordecai in the morning, give him my royal robes and my royal horse, and you, Haman, shall lead the horse and make sure everyone bows down to him."

Haman was furious.

"I detest that Mordecai," he told his wife.

"Well, do something about it," she said.

Haman went and built a huge gallows on which he planned to hang Mordecai on the appointed day.

The next evening, Ahasuerus and Haman had dinner with the queen. It was a sumptuous affair and they both enjoyed themselves thoroughly. But Esther looked so sad that the king remarked:

"I will do anything you ask to make you happy."

"My Lord," she said, "there are in your kingdom a certain people, loyal and devoted to you. An evil man has decreed they should be killed. They are Jews, my Lord, and I am one of them."

"That is terrible!" exclaimed the king. "I do not want you to be killed. Who is behind all this?"

"Haman," she said.

"I will not have it," the king cried. "We will have to change the decree. Haman! You are the one who will be killed."

Ahasuerus allowed the Jews to fight against anyone who attacked them. On the allotted day there was a big battle which the Jews won.

Haman was hanged on the gallows he had built for Mordecai, and Mordecai became prime minister instead. Esther lived happily ever after, as did king Ahasuerus. As for the Jews, they still celebrate the defeat of the wicked Haman every year on Purim or the Festival of Lots.

The Ignorant Shepherd Boy

This is the story of a poor shepherd boy who lived with his father in the mountains of Poland. He knew nothing of the world and had never learned to read or write. When he was thirteen, his father took him to the synagogue for the first time.

The boy entered the synagogue timidly. It was a simple building, but he thought it was beautiful. All the candles were lit. The Ark was adorned with wood carvings, and the scrolls inside were clothed in white satin and silver. It was the Day of Atonement.

The Rabbi and the congregation were dressed in white and as they stood, they sang a strange, sad tune. The boy wanted to join in, but he did not know the words. He looked at his prayer book but he could make no sense of it. Oh, how he wished he could read! How he wished he could sing those sad songs and offer prayers to God.

The service on the Day of Atonement lasts all day. From dawn till dusk the boy sat still, watching and listening to the wonderful sights and sounds around him. In a few moments three stars would appear in the sky, a sign that the service should end. He had to do something! Something to show that he too could sing praises to God. His hand reached inside his pocket.

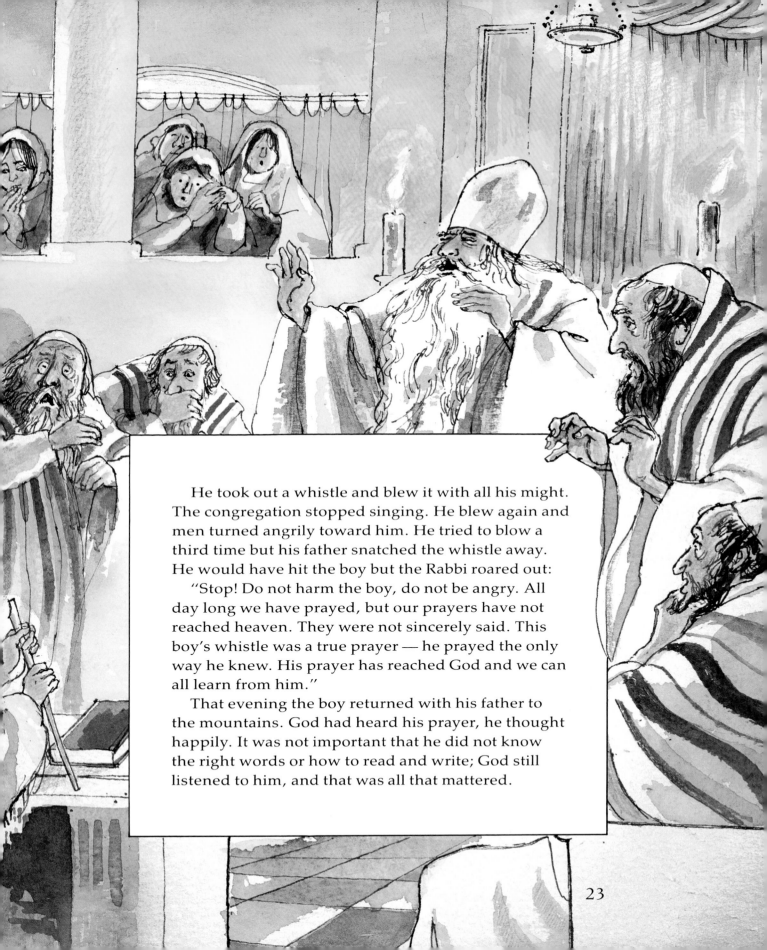

He took out a whistle and blew it with all his might. The congregation stopped singing. He blew again and men turned angrily toward him. He tried to blow a third time but his father snatched the whistle away. He would have hit the boy but the Rabbi roared out:

"Stop! Do not harm the boy, do not be angry. All day long we have prayed, but our prayers have not reached heaven. They were not sincerely said. This boy's whistle was a true prayer — he prayed the only way he knew. His prayer has reached God and we can all learn from him."

That evening the boy returned with his father to the mountains. God had heard his prayer, he thought happily. It was not important that he did not know the right words or how to read and write; God still listened to him, and that was all that mattered.

23

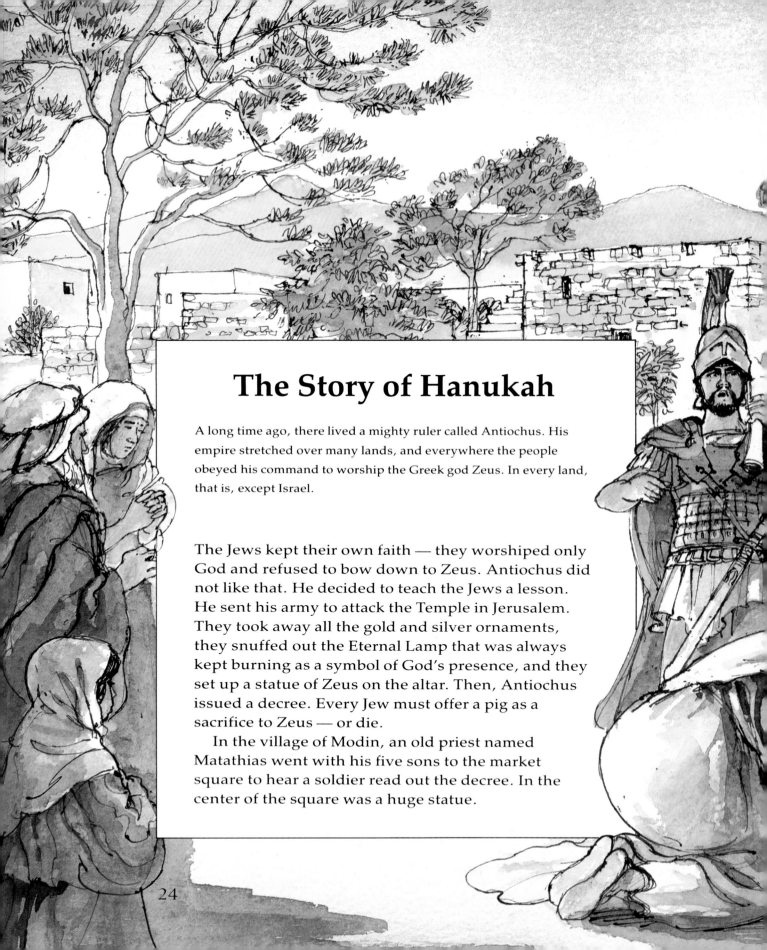

The Story of Hanukah

A long time ago, there lived a mighty ruler called Antiochus. His empire stretched over many lands, and everywhere the people obeyed his command to worship the Greek god Zeus. In every land, that is, except Israel.

The Jews kept their own faith — they worshiped only God and refused to bow down to Zeus. Antiochus did not like that. He decided to teach the Jews a lesson. He sent his army to attack the Temple in Jerusalem. They took away all the gold and silver ornaments, they snuffed out the Eternal Lamp that was always kept burning as a symbol of God's presence, and they set up a statue of Zeus on the altar. Then, Antiochus issued a decree. Every Jew must offer a pig as a sacrifice to Zeus — or die.

In the village of Modin, an old priest named Matathias went with his five sons to the market square to hear a soldier read out the decree. In the center of the square was a huge statue.

24

"Who will be the first to worship Zeus?" the soldier asked.

There was much muttering and mumbling. No one wanted to sacrifice, but no one wanted to die either.

Finally one man came forward and bowed down to the statue. Up leaped Matathias! He grabbed a sword and killed the man.

"What the...?" the soldier began. But he could say no more — Matathias had killed him too.

"Whoever is for God," he shouted, "follow me!"

Matathias, with his sons and many of the villagers, ran into the hills to hide. Word spread quickly, and soon others joined them; all of them ready to defy Antiochus and worship God. They hid in the mountains by day. At night, they crept out to ambush army patrols and to tear down the statues of Zeus.

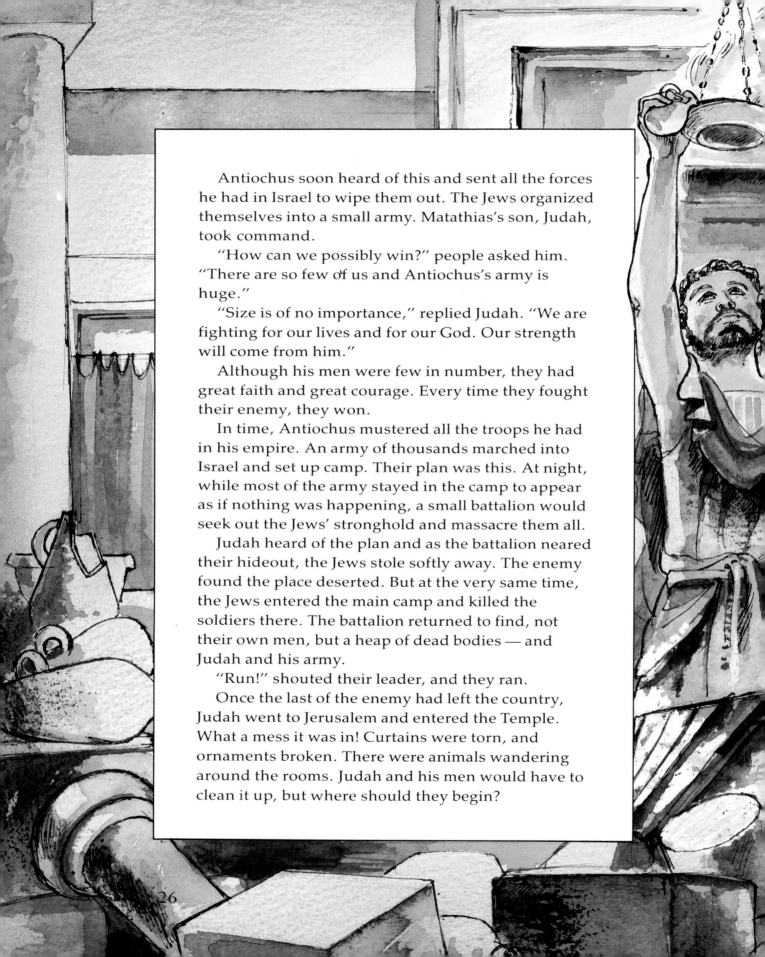

Antiochus soon heard of this and sent all the forces he had in Israel to wipe them out. The Jews organized themselves into a small army. Matathias's son, Judah, took command.

"How can we possibly win?" people asked him. "There are so few of us and Antiochus's army is huge."

"Size is of no importance," replied Judah. "We are fighting for our lives and for our God. Our strength will come from him."

Although his men were few in number, they had great faith and great courage. Every time they fought their enemy, they won.

In time, Antiochus mustered all the troops he had in his empire. An army of thousands marched into Israel and set up camp. Their plan was this. At night, while most of the army stayed in the camp to appear as if nothing was happening, a small battalion would seek out the Jews' stronghold and massacre them all.

Judah heard of the plan and as the battalion neared their hideout, the Jews stole softly away. The enemy found the place deserted. But at the very same time, the Jews entered the main camp and killed the soldiers there. The battalion returned to find, not their own men, but a heap of dead bodies — and Judah and his army.

"Run!" shouted their leader, and they ran.

Once the last of the enemy had left the country, Judah went to Jerusalem and entered the Temple. What a mess it was in! Curtains were torn, and ornaments broken. There were animals wandering around the rooms. Judah and his men would have to clean it up, but where should they begin?

"The first thing to be done," said Judah, "is to light the Eternal Lamp."

He soon found it, but could find no oil with which to light it. All the jars of oil had been overturned, leaving a sticky mess on the floor. He searched and searched without any success.

Then, in a corner, he saw a tiny jug. It had a little oil in it — enough to keep the lamp burning for a day. What was Judah to do? Fresh oil supplies were four days' journey away. He could wait till more oil was brought, or light the lamp now and hope for the best.

"We should celebrate God's triumph now," he said, and lit the lamp.

Then a strange thing happened. The amount of oil in the lamp was tiny — but it kept on burning. It burned for eight days — long enough for the new supplies to arrive.

Some say this was a miracle. Others say a greater miracle was the fact that Judah and his small group of followers could conquer the huge army of Antiochus. As the Bible itself tells us:

"'Not by might, but by My Spirit,' says the Lord."

27

The Fox and the Grapes

This is a story about a foolish fox, but it could also tell us something about what happens when people get too greedy.

One day the fox was walking along a dusty lane, when he passed by a vineyard, with vines full of large bunches of grapes. The fox was very fond of grapes and these were so ripe and inviting that he decided to creep inside and eat as many as he could. The vineyard was surrounded by a high fence and the gate was locked — how was he to get in?

"Perhaps," he said to himself, "I shall find a gap in the fence through which I can squeeze."

He spent the next hour walking around the vineyard. He found a small hole in the fence.

"If I breathe in very hard," he thought, "I can just get through." But it was no good, he was too fat.

"If I do not eat anything for a day, I shall grow thinner," he said.

For a whole day he ate nothing and drank nothing, but still could not squeeze through.

"Maybe another day of fasting would make a difference," he thought. All the next day he sat by the gap in the fence without food or water, then he tried again.

"Almost, almost!" he cried. "Just one more day without food or water is all I need."

By the end of the third day he was weak with hunger, but he easily slipped through the hole.

What a sight greeted him! Row upon row of vines covered with black grapes as big as plums. The fox had a feast. All the next day he ate and the next day, and the next. Then he returned to the hole in the fence. He tried to get out, but he could not. He had grown too fat.

"Oh dear!" he exclaimed, "I shall have to lose weight quickly. Perhaps if I fast for a day I shall be thin enough again."

He fasted one day, but it was not enough. He fasted a second day, but he was still too large for the hole.

"Just one more day," he said, "and surely I shall make it."

He fasted a third day, and by the evening he could climb back out of the vineyard.

Tired and faint with hunger, the fox continued his walk along the dusty lane.

29

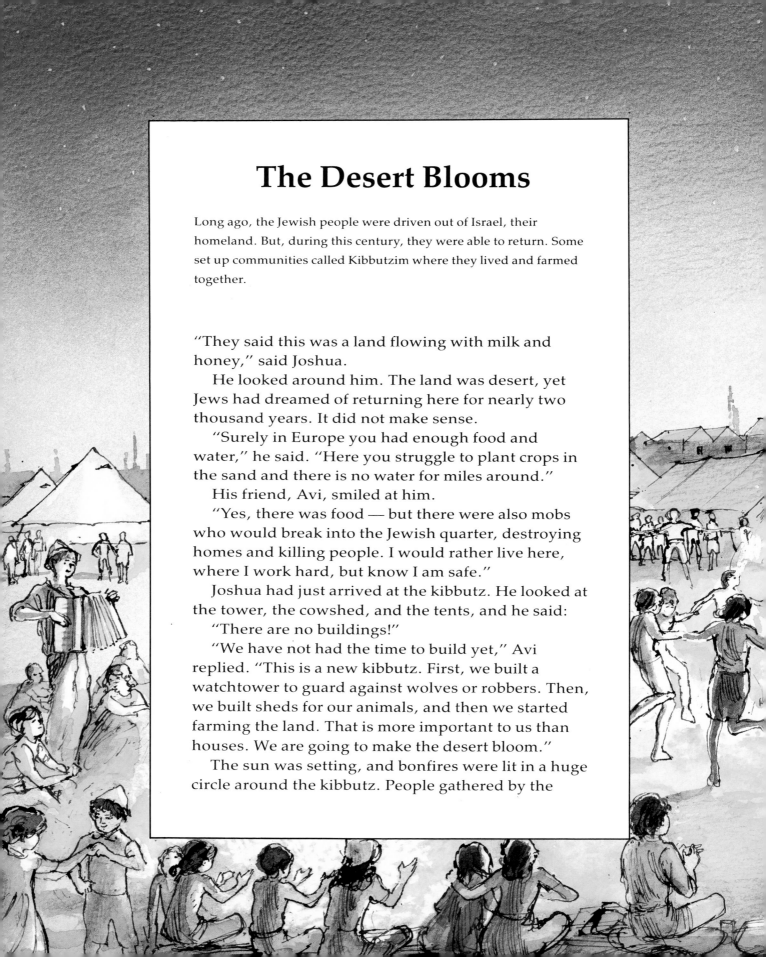

The Desert Blooms

Long ago, the Jewish people were driven out of Israel, their homeland. But, during this century, they were able to return. Some set up communities called Kibbutzim where they lived and farmed together.

"They said this was a land flowing with milk and honey," said Joshua.

He looked around him. The land was desert, yet Jews had dreamed of returning here for nearly two thousand years. It did not make sense.

"Surely in Europe you had enough food and water," he said. "Here you struggle to plant crops in the sand and there is no water for miles around."

His friend, Avi, smiled at him.

"Yes, there was food — but there were also mobs who would break into the Jewish quarter, destroying homes and killing people. I would rather live here, where I work hard, but know I am safe."

Joshua had just arrived at the kibbutz. He looked at the tower, the cowshed, and the tents, and he said:

"There are no buildings!"

"We have not had the time to build yet," Avi replied. "This is a new kibbutz. First, we built a watchtower to guard against wolves or robbers. Then, we built sheds for our animals, and then we started farming the land. That is more important to us than houses. We are going to make the desert bloom."

The sun was setting, and bonfires were lit in a huge circle around the kibbutz. People gathered by the

fires. They told each other stories about the ancient
heroes of Israel, and they sang songs of their hopes
for the future. It was dark now, and the sky was full of
brilliant stars.

"Let us sleep out in the open tonight," said Avi.

"Is it safe?" Joshua asked.

"Of course!" Avi replied, "the place is guarded."

As he lay down, Joshua saw men and women with
guns, walking around the circle of fires.

Joshua was almost asleep when shots were fired
and the tower lit up the camp. People were running to
the shed. There were more shots, a howl, and then
silence. A wolf had gotten in, but it had been killed.

Avi breathed a sigh of relief. "It is dangerous here,
but so beautiful! Look at those stars!"

Joshua agreed. It was like a dream — sleeping
outside in a desert. Could it bloom one day?

That was fifty years ago. Today the desert is full of
trees, grasses, and flowers. The dream has come true.

The Golem of Prague

The Jewish people have had a sad history. They have often been blamed for crimes they did not commit, driven from their homes, and even killed. This story tells of those times.

Rabbi Judah Lev was a very holy man. He lived happily in Prague until the Jews there were accused of killing children and using their blood in worship. It was a lie, but people who hated Jews pretended it was true. Every time someone disappeared, Rabbi Judah would have to go to the court room and prove that the Jews had not hurt them.

One night, he prayed hard to God.

"Oh Lord," he said, "please help me to stop these terrible lies." He put a piece of paper under his pillow and went to sleep. In the morning, he found writing on the paper.

"Make a man," it said. "He will help you. He will do everything you ask, but you must never use him as a servant, and you must destroy him when he has fulfilled your wishes."

At midnight, Rabbi Judah went out into the marshes. He drew the figure of a huge man in the mud and wrote the secret name of God on his forehead. He said some special prayers and the man immediately sprang to life. Rabbi Judah called him "Yossel the Golem."

Now, at that time there lived a Baron who spent his time and money drinking and gambling. He lived with his stepdaughter, Maria, in a tumbledown castle. Maria was very rich, and the Baron hated her. He hoped she would die so that he could have her money.

One day, he locked Maria in the cellar, then he went to the police.

"My daughter, my darling daughter," he sobbed. "She has been killed by the Jews."

The Jewish leaders were arrested and put on trial. The Judge heard the evidence. The Jews denied the story.

"Guilty!" roared the Judge. "You are all sentenced to death."

Just then, the door of the court flew open and in walked Yossel the Golem, carrying little Maria.

"Father, father," she cried, "why did you lock me in the cellar?"

The Baron admitted the plot, and the Jews were freed at once.

Rabbi Judah thanked God.

"Now I must destroy the Golem," he thought. He looked at Yossel as he slept. "But not just yet — he is so big and strong he could help around the house."

"Yossel!" he called. "I want you to carry water from the well to the tank in the kitchen."

The Golem did as he was told, and Rabbi Judah went to his room to study. Two hours later, Yossel was still carrying water, although the tank was overflowing!

"Stop!" the Rabbi shouted, and Yossel stopped.

"I really must destroy him," he thought. "But not just yet."

Time passed and Yossel grew more active. Instead of lying asleep till the Rabbi gave him an order, he got up and walked around. People ran away when they saw him — he was so big and strange.

"You must destroy him," they begged the Rabbi.

"Alas, it is not so easy. I have to erase the name of God from his forehead, I should have done it when he lay asleep. Now, he does not sleep at all and he is too tall for anyone to reach."

Yossel found a family at supper. He ate all their food, the plates, the knives, the glasses — then he ate the table.

The Rabbi thought of a plan. If Yossel liked food, perhaps he would like drink.

"I need a volunteer," he said. "Someone brave."

A young girl named Miriam spoke up. "I will do it," she said. Miriam took the Golem into her home.

"Have some wine," she said, and gave him a glass. Yossel drank the glass of wine, then snatched the bottle from Miriam and drank that. He opened another bottle and another. He found some large barrels in the cellar and drank them all. Yossel smiled, then he fell over and went to sleep. Miriam quickly rubbed out the secret name on his forehead. At once he disappeared and all that was left of him was a heap of mud.

Everyone thanked Miriam, and Rabbi Judah offered prayers to God.

"Never again, O Lord," he prayed, "will I disobey your commands."

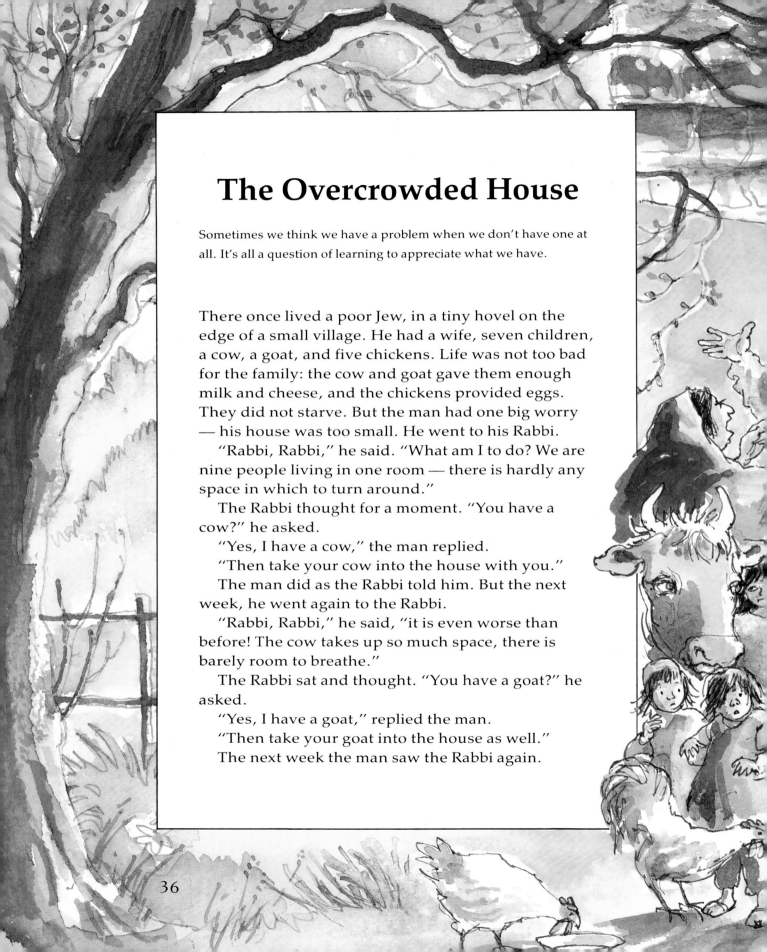

The Overcrowded House

Sometimes we think we have a problem when we don't have one at all. It's all a question of learning to appreciate what we have.

There once lived a poor Jew, in a tiny hovel on the edge of a small village. He had a wife, seven children, a cow, a goat, and five chickens. Life was not too bad for the family: the cow and goat gave them enough milk and cheese, and the chickens provided eggs. They did not starve. But the man had one big worry — his house was too small. He went to his Rabbi.

"Rabbi, Rabbi," he said. "What am I to do? We are nine people living in one room — there is hardly any space in which to turn around."

The Rabbi thought for a moment. "You have a cow?" he asked.

"Yes, I have a cow," the man replied.

"Then take your cow into the house with you."

The man did as the Rabbi told him. But the next week, he went again to the Rabbi.

"Rabbi, Rabbi," he said, "it is even worse than before! The cow takes up so much space, there is barely room to breathe."

The Rabbi sat and thought. "You have a goat?" he asked.

"Yes, I have a goat," replied the man.

"Then take your goat into the house as well."

The next week the man saw the Rabbi again.

"Rabbi, Rabbi," he said, "it is even worse now that the goat is in the house, she smells so."

"You have chickens?"

"Yes," said the man, "I have chickens."

"Well then," said the Rabbi, " take the chickens into the house also."

The next week the man knocked once more on the Rabbi's door.

"Rabbi, Rabbi, I cannot stand this any longer! Five chickens flying around the house — the feathers get everywhere — and the noise! You should hear it! It is unbearable. What am I to do?"

The Rabbi sat and thought.

"You should take the cow, the goat, and the chickens out of your house and put them back where they were before."

The next week, the man did not go to see the Rabbi, but the Rabbi saw him, praying happily in the synagogue.

"Well?" the Rabbi asked. "How is it now at home?"

"Oh Rabbi," said the man, "it is wonderful! Now that I have taken out the cow, the goat, and the chickens, there is so much room!"

Helm

Helm is a very special town. The people there are famous for being stupid, though they think they are very wise. They are also very honest, and they never go back on their word.

Shloime and his wife Gittel went to bed one night, and left the front door open.

"You must go and close the door," Shloime said.

"No, you must close it," said Gittel to Shloime.

"I cannot do that," said Shloime. "I said you must close it, and I never go back on my word."

"But I never go back on my word either," said Gittel.

They agreed that the first person to speak should close the door. They lay in silence. The wind howled through the house. Icicles formed on the bedstead; snowflakes settled on the blankets. Neither spoke.

A band of robbers entered the house. They took all the copper saucepans and the silver candlesticks. Gittel said not a word. They took all the books and the clock. Shloime sat still.

"I am hungry," one of the robbers said, "let us have a bite to eat." They lit a fire and ate as much food as they could. Then they took the table, and the chairs; the stove and the carpets. They took the bookcases and the curtains; the wallpaper and the window-frames. Shloime and Gittel remained silent. The thieves left, their hands so full of loot, they could not close the door.

The next morning, Gittel went out early to find
food. Shloime sat on the floor. A traveling barber saw
the open door and walked in.

"Do you need a hair cut?" he asked.

Shloime said nothing so the barber cut his hair.
"Well, how do you like it?" he said when he had
finished. Shloime did not answer, so the barber cut off
some more.

"You know, it might be better to shave it off
completely," the barber said. Shloime did not want
his head shaved, but he was not going to speak. The
barber shaved his head.

"Now," said the barber, "you owe me ten kopeks."

Shloime had no money. He said nothing.

"What! You won't pay me?" shouted the barber.
He went to the fireplace, gathered some soot and
smeared it all over Shloime's face. Still, Shloime did
not utter a sound. The barber stormed out of the
house, leaving the door open.

Some time later, Gittel returned. She saw her
husband sitting on the floor, with a bald head and
sooty face, and screamed.

"My poor Shloime! What have they done to you?"

Shloime stood up, triumphant. "You spoke first!"
he said. "Now go and close the door."

Hannah Senesh

In September 1939, eighteen-year-old Hannah Senesh left her home in Hungary and boarded a boat for Palestine. Hannah was sad to leave her family and her friends, but she knew that in Hungary, she could never go to the university or get a good job, because she was a Jew and at that time, life was very hard for the Jews.

The Second World War had just started. Hitler's German army was marching through Europe and Hungary was his ally. The Germans rounded up all the Jews, and put them in prisons or concentration camps. To get away, Hannah Senesh, like many young Jews, went to Palestine — the land called Israel in the Bible. They hoped to build a new Israel there, where Jews could live freely and not be persecuted.

In Palestine, Hannah learned to be a farmer. She spent her days picking oranges and milking cows, but she heard much about the war in Europe. Her mother wrote to her and told her how her brother George had escaped to Paris and hoped to join Hannah soon. Hannah asked her mother to come too, but she replied she could not leave.

"I am happy though, that my children are safe," she said.

At that time, Palestine was ruled by Britain. Some of the Jews there joined the British army to fight against the Germans and Hannah volunteered for the Air Force.

In March 1944 she set off with six others on a daring mission. They were dropped by parachute into Yugoslavia, where they rescued British soldiers held prisoner by the Germans. Then, they moved on, crossing the border into Hungary. Their aim was to help the Jews escape from the clutches of the Nazis. But soon, Hannah was caught by German soldiers and sent to prison.

Soldiers beat her and tortured her, but she would not tell them what her mission was.

One day, the Commandant sent for her.

"We have a surprise for you," he said. Hannah was pushed into the next room and there she saw her mother!

"Hannah!" her mother cried, "I thought you were safe in Palestine. Why did you come back to this terrible place?"

"Do not ask me," Hannah replied. "They have tortured me for the secret — if I tell you they will torture you, too."

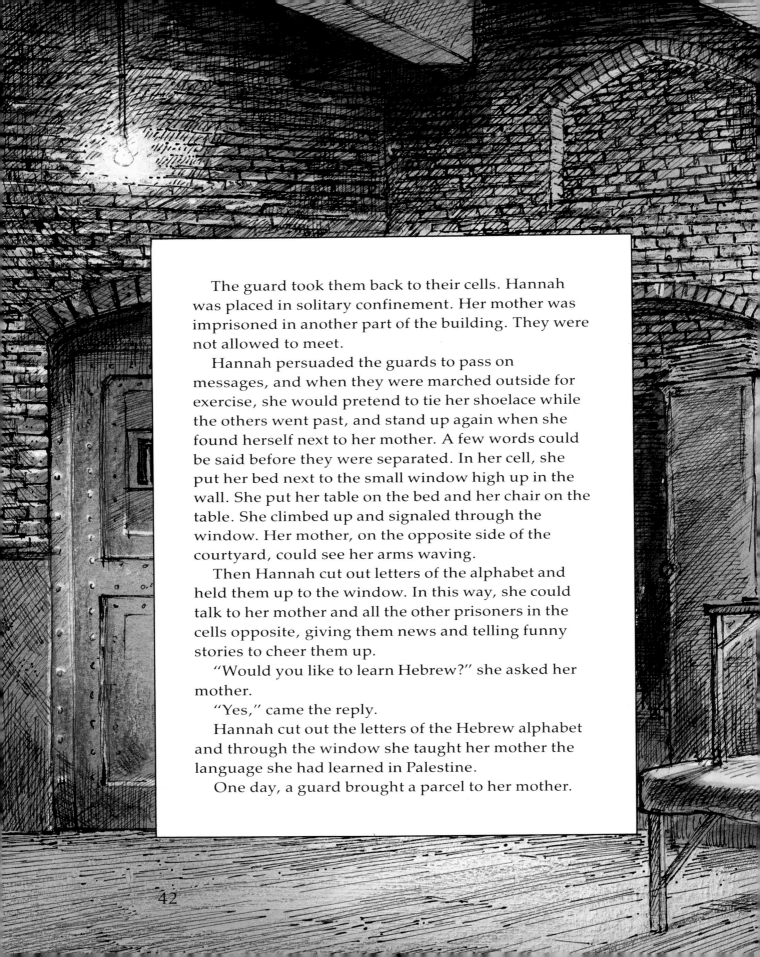

The guard took them back to their cells. Hannah was placed in solitary confinement. Her mother was imprisoned in another part of the building. They were not allowed to meet.

Hannah persuaded the guards to pass on messages, and when they were marched outside for exercise, she would pretend to tie her shoelace while the others went past, and stand up again when she found herself next to her mother. A few words could be said before they were separated. In her cell, she put her bed next to the small window high up in the wall. She put her table on the bed and her chair on the table. She climbed up and signaled through the window. Her mother, on the opposite side of the courtyard, could see her arms waving.

Then Hannah cut out letters of the alphabet and held them up to the window. In this way, she could talk to her mother and all the other prisoners in the cells opposite, giving them news and telling funny stories to cheer them up.

"Would you like to learn Hebrew?" she asked her mother.

"Yes," came the reply.

Hannah cut out the letters of the Hebrew alphabet and through the window she taught her mother the language she had learned in Palestine.

One day, a guard brought a parcel to her mother.

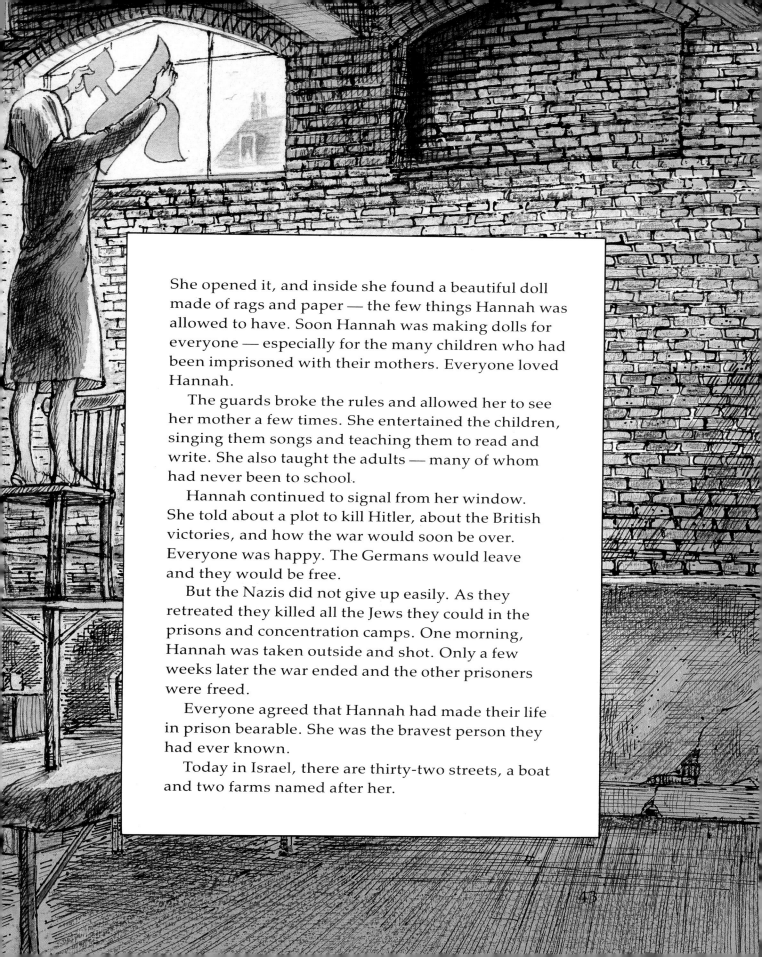

She opened it, and inside she found a beautiful doll made of rags and paper — the few things Hannah was allowed to have. Soon Hannah was making dolls for everyone — especially for the many children who had been imprisoned with their mothers. Everyone loved Hannah.

The guards broke the rules and allowed her to see her mother a few times. She entertained the children, singing them songs and teaching them to read and write. She also taught the adults — many of whom had never been to school.

Hannah continued to signal from her window. She told about a plot to kill Hitler, about the British victories, and how the war would soon be over. Everyone was happy. The Germans would leave and they would be free.

But the Nazis did not give up easily. As they retreated they killed all the Jews they could in the prisons and concentration camps. One morning, Hannah was taken outside and shot. Only a few weeks later the war ended and the other prisoners were freed.

Everyone agreed that Hannah had made their life in prison bearable. She was the bravest person they had ever known.

Today in Israel, there are thirty-two streets, a boat and two farms named after her.

Background Notes

Abraham and the Idols
According to Jewish tradition, Abraham was the first person to believe in one God, yet the Bible is strangely silent on how he came to that momentous discovery. Therefore, countless stories developed over the centuries, recounting Abraham's childhood and youth in order to fill the gap. Such tales were used for teaching purposes and are part of a collection known as *Midrash*.

The Lie and Evil Enter the Ark
This is another *Midrash*. It seeks to explain why, despite the destruction wrought by the flood, the world remained as evil and corrupt as it had been before.

Akiva, the Donkey, the Rooster, and the Candle
Rabbi Akiva, c.50–135 CE, was the greatest scholar of his generation. He lived as a shepherd, and was allegedly illiterate until the age of forty. Though a major contributor to the systemization of Jewish law, he had great popular appeal and his poverty and simple manner gave rise to many stories about him. This one is found in the *Talmud*, the major work on Jewish law written in the 6th century.

Torah: the Hebrew term for the first five books of the Bible.

The Story of Esther
This is the only biblical story included in the book. It has significance for Jews as the prime example of racial prejudice and its consequences. Throughout Jewish history there have been repeated attempts to massacre and exterminate them, so deliverance and survival are themes of great importance to Jews the world over.

The redemption from Haman is celebrated each year by reading the story of Esther. Whenever Haman is mentioned, Jews use rattles and other noise-makers, shout and stamp their feet to "blot out" the accursed name.

The Ignorant Shepherd Boy
Hassidism developed in the 18th century partly as a reaction against the heavy emphasis in Judaism on scholarly learning. It stressed sincerity of feeling and devotion through joy rather than learning, and this tale sums up the essence of that belief. The movement still flourishes today; the Hassidim are distinctive in that many wear the same clothes of their 18th century forebears — black coats, broad-brimmed hats, and long sidelocks.

The Day of Atonement (Yom Kippur) takes place at the beginning of October, although the exact date changes each year. It is a fast day, lasting 25 hours from sunset to nightfall.

The Ark is the focal point in a synagogue. It contains the *Torah*, handwritten on scrolls of parchment.

How Judah Saved the Jews
The Jewish revolt against Syria led by Judah in 168 BCE is celebrated during an eight day festival called Hanukah. The events described in the story are based on the First Book of Maccabees in the Apocrypha, though the miracle with the oil is a later story.

This was one of many incidents that occurred because Jewish worship had been prohibited, and during the persecution, Judaism gained many martyrs. The quotation from Zechariah 4:6; "Not by might...but by My Spirit" became a message of hope to Jews in times of persecution, and is a comment on Jewish survival despite extraordinary odds.

The Fox and the Grapes

Another period of persecution was that of the Romans during the 2nd century CE. Since it was not politic to criticize the rulers openly, the use of fables became a popular means to put forward a point of view. The Romans were notorious for their greed, yet many Jews wished to emulate them; this story is directed at such people, pointing out the futility of such a way of life. The fox at the end of the story is three days hungrier than he was when he first saw the grapes.

The Desert Blooms

Many stories are told to children in Israel today about the Halutsim (pioneer) Jews from Russia and central Europe who came to Palestine as farmers from the 1880s onward.

On the kibbutz, most goods and land were held in common. This was not only the result of many socialist and communist ideas the immigrants brought with them, but also the safest and most successful way to farm for a people who arrived with little experience of such work, and no money.

The Golem of Prague

Rabbi Judah Lev (or Loew) of Prague (1525–1609) was a scholar and mathematician, famous in both the Jewish and non-Jewish worlds of the time.

A golem is an imaginary creature, a body without a soul, created artificially from the earth and brought to life through a series of mystical prayers. Since only God can create a soul, the golem is an imperfect being, incapable of speech or independent thought.

Legends about golems originate in the *Talmud*, but it is in the Middle Ages that they became popular, taking on many features of local folklore and fairy tales.

The Overcrowded House

Poverty has been a feature of Jewish life throughout the ages. In most societies, Jews were second-class citizens, often forbidden to own land or practice certain trades. This was usually accepted with a quiet resignation. Jews developed a wry sense of humor which helped ease the situation a little and they were very good at laughing at themselves. This story is typical of Eastern European humor.

Helm

Every culture has its "idiots;" in Jewish Eastern Europe they lived in Helm, a small town in Poland. The people of Helm are not really stupid, they follow a stubborn logic of their own, regardless of what experience and the world teaches. Hence, they conclude that a spoon stirred in tea sweetens it, and sugar is only added to tell you how long to keep stirring.

Helm stories are satirical. We laugh at Shloime and Gittel, their stubbornness and lack of any sense of proportion, but really we behave no differently.

Hannah Senesh

Two events are important for the understanding of modern Jewry: the holocaust and the establishment of the state of Israel. This story, a biography rather than a legend, has been included as it touches on both. Hannah Senesh is a national folk hero in Israel where she has captured the imagination of young people for two generations. Her poetry is well known, and some poems set to music have been popular hits.

A note about dates

Because of the Christian nature of the terms BC and AD, Jews usually refer to dates as BCE or CE: that is, Before the Common Era and Common Era.